About
Skill Builders
Math

by R. B. Snow and Clareen Nelson-Arnold

Welcome to RBP Books' Skill Builders series. Like our Summer Bridge Activities collection, the Skill Builders series is designed to make learning both fun and rewarding.

Skill Builders Math provides students with focused practice to help them reinforce and develop math skills. Each Skill Builders volume is grade-level appropriate, with clear examples and instructions on each page to guide the lesson. In accordance with NCTM standards, exercises for grade three cover a variety of math skills, including addition, subtraction, multiplication, division, word problems, shapes, time, money values, fractions, and decimals.

A critical thinking section includes exercises to develop higher-order thinking skills.

Learning is more effective when approached with an element of fun and enthusiasm—just as most children approach life. That's why the Skill Builders combine entertaining and academically sound exercises and fun themes to make reviewing basic skills fun and effective, for both you and your budding scholars.

D1318687

Table of Contents

Addition and Subtraction without Regrouping

Solve each problem below.

1. $10 - 6 =$ __4__ $2 + 3 =$ _____ $1 + 9 =$ _____

2. $5 + 2 =$ _3_ $15 - 5 =$ _____ $16 - 7 =$ _____

3. $17 - 5 =$ _12_ $14 + 2 =$ _____ $3 + 6 =$ _____

4. $11 - 6 =$ _5_ $9 - 3 =$ _____ $10 + 7 =$ _____

5. $10 + 3 =$ _13_ $9 - 9 =$ _____ $9 + 3 =$ _____

6. $12 - 4 =$ _____ $6 + 6 =$ _____ $15 - 4 =$ _____

7. $8 + 7 =$ _____ $15 - 6 =$ _____ $11 + 6 =$ _____

8. $11 - 4 =$ _____ $14 - 7 =$ _____ $8 + 4 =$ _____

9. $13 - 9 =$ _____ $7 + 2 =$ _____ $6 + 8 =$ _____

10. $7 + 7 =$ _____ $15 - 2 =$ _____ $11 - 3 =$ _____

11. $18 - 3 =$ _____ $2 + 5 =$ _____ $3 + 4 =$ _____

12. $16 + 2 =$ _____ $16 - 3 =$ _____ $9 - 4 =$ _____

13. $14 + 2 =$ _____ $17 - 5 =$ _____ $4 + 8 =$ _____

14. $3 + 6 =$ _____ $15 - 4 =$ _____ $10 - 7 =$ _____

15. $10 - 8 =$ _____ $12 - 5 =$ _____ $18 - 4 =$ _____

16. $14 - 4 =$ _____ $8 + 5 =$ _____ $3 + 3 =$ _____

Addition and Subtraction without Regrouping

Solve each problem below.

1.
$$\begin{array}{r} 1 \\ +\,8 \\ \hline \mathbf{9} \end{array} \quad \begin{array}{r} 16 \\ -\,6 \\ \hline \end{array} \quad \begin{array}{r} 15 \\ -\,0 \\ \hline \end{array} \quad \begin{array}{r} 4 \\ +\,11 \\ \hline \end{array} \quad \begin{array}{r} 15 \\ +\,1 \\ \hline \end{array}$$

2.
$$\begin{array}{r} 5 \\ +\,8 \\ \hline \end{array} \quad \begin{array}{r} 3 \\ +\,11 \\ \hline \end{array} \quad \begin{array}{r} 18 \\ -\,9 \\ \hline \end{array} \quad \begin{array}{r} 9 \\ +\,5 \\ \hline \end{array} \quad \begin{array}{r} 16 \\ -\,7 \\ \hline \end{array}$$

3.
$$\begin{array}{r} 17 \\ -\,1 \\ \hline \end{array} \quad \begin{array}{r} 18 \\ -\,0 \\ \hline \end{array} \quad \begin{array}{r} 11 \\ +\,4 \\ \hline \end{array} \quad \begin{array}{r} 7 \\ +\,6 \\ \hline \end{array} \quad \begin{array}{r} 14 \\ -\,9 \\ \hline \end{array}$$

4.
$$\begin{array}{r} 18 \\ -\,4 \\ \hline \end{array} \quad \begin{array}{r} 11 \\ -\,3 \\ \hline \end{array} \quad \begin{array}{r} 8 \\ +\,8 \\ \hline \end{array} \quad \begin{array}{r} 16 \\ -\,9 \\ \hline \end{array} \quad \begin{array}{r} 14 \\ -\,5 \\ \hline \end{array}$$

5.
$$\begin{array}{r} 14 \\ +\,4 \\ \hline \end{array} \quad \begin{array}{r} 15 \\ -\,2 \\ \hline \end{array} \quad \begin{array}{r} 8 \\ +\,9 \\ \hline \end{array} \quad \begin{array}{r} 18 \\ -\,6 \\ \hline \end{array} \quad \begin{array}{r} 6 \\ +\,9 \\ \hline \end{array}$$

6.
$$\begin{array}{r} 10 \\ +\,3 \\ \hline \end{array} \quad \begin{array}{r} 11 \\ -\,7 \\ \hline \end{array} \quad \begin{array}{r} 14 \\ -\,9 \\ \hline \end{array} \quad \begin{array}{r} 13 \\ +\,5 \\ \hline \end{array} \quad \begin{array}{r} 15 \\ -\,9 \\ \hline \end{array}$$

Solve each problem below.

1.

2	6	4	5	7
8	4	4	5	7
+ 3	+ 3	+ 3	+ 5	+ 3
13				

2.

5	4	2	7	8
3	8	9	5	2
4	2	1	3	5
+ 1	+ 1	+ 3	+ 3	+ 3

3.

3	4	9	6	7
7	8	1	6	8
5	2	5	3	1
+ 1	+ 3	+ 2	+ 3	+ 2

Be careful! Column addition can be dangerous!

Odd and Even Star Puzzle

Follow the instructions underneath the puzzle to complete this exercise. Have fun!

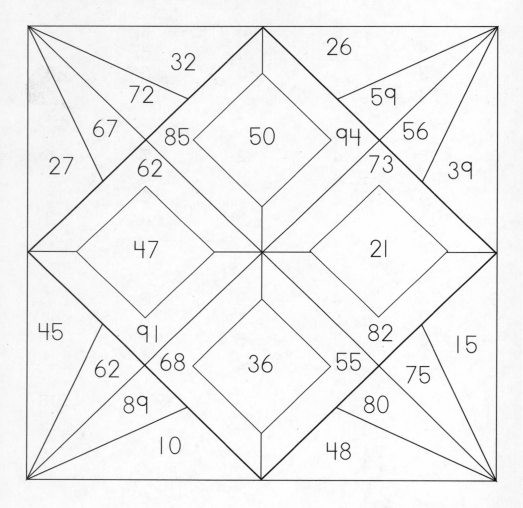

Color the even numbers between 2 and 50 blue.
Color the odd numbers between 1 and 49 green.
Color the even numbers between 52 and 100 orange.
Color the odd numbers between 51 and 99 yellow.

2- and 3-Digit Addition without Regrouping

Solve each problem below.

1.

23	64	47	13	55
+ 42	+ 25	+ 31	+ 45	+ 30
65				

2.

74	58	26	35	12
+ 23	+ 41	+ 33	+ 54	+ 77

3.

52	36	15	18	84
+ 37	+ 23	+ 72	+ 81	+ 12

4.

352	475	724	650	298
+ 436	+ 510	+143	+ 227	+ 500

5.

525	631	447	319	752
+ 261	+ 155	+ 432	+ 450	+ 136

2- and 3-Digit Subtraction without Regrouping

Solve each problem below.

1.
$$\begin{array}{r} 86 \\ -\ 32 \\ \hline \mathbf{54} \end{array}$$
$$\begin{array}{r} 52 \\ -\ 12 \\ \hline \end{array}$$
$$\begin{array}{r} 67 \\ -\ 45 \\ \hline \end{array}$$
$$\begin{array}{r} 95 \\ -\ 30 \\ \hline \end{array}$$
$$\begin{array}{r} 87 \\ -\ 26 \\ \hline \end{array}$$

2.
$$\begin{array}{r} 38 \\ -\ 14 \\ \hline \end{array}$$
$$\begin{array}{r} 75 \\ -\ 52 \\ \hline \end{array}$$
$$\begin{array}{r} 88 \\ -\ 37 \\ \hline \end{array}$$
$$\begin{array}{r} 74 \\ -\ 24 \\ \hline \end{array}$$
$$\begin{array}{r} 47 \\ -\ 15 \\ \hline \end{array}$$

3.
$$\begin{array}{r} 57 \\ -\ 33 \\ \hline \end{array}$$
$$\begin{array}{r} 49 \\ -\ 25 \\ \hline \end{array}$$
$$\begin{array}{r} 36 \\ -\ 14 \\ \hline \end{array}$$
$$\begin{array}{r} 87 \\ -\ 77 \\ \hline \end{array}$$
$$\begin{array}{r} 70 \\ -\ 30 \\ \hline \end{array}$$

4.
$$\begin{array}{r} 497 \\ -\ 225 \\ \hline \end{array}$$
$$\begin{array}{r} 564 \\ -\ 423 \\ \hline \end{array}$$
$$\begin{array}{r} 372 \\ -\ 222 \\ \hline \end{array}$$

Those numbers are pretty BIG but you can handle them!

5.
$$\begin{array}{r} 283 \\ -\ 220 \\ \hline \end{array}$$
$$\begin{array}{r} 488 \\ -\ 351 \\ \hline \end{array}$$
$$\begin{array}{r} 695 \\ -\ 233 \\ \hline \end{array}$$

6.
$$\begin{array}{r} 348 \\ -\ 33 \\ \hline \end{array}$$
$$\begin{array}{r} 996 \\ -\ 73 \\ \hline \end{array}$$
$$\begin{array}{r} 465 \\ -\ 50 \\ \hline \end{array}$$

Addition and Subtraction: Space Adventure

Start from the center numeral and work outward to answer each problem.

Check yourself with a calculator!

Math Grade 3—RBP3489

Addition with Regrouping

Solve the problems below.

1.
```
  1
 27      39      46      57      49
+ 24    + 53    + 37    + 29    + 15
 51
```

2.
```
 75      93      58      64      86
+ 19    +  7    + 34    + 28    + 17
```

3.
```
 66      79      43      56      98
+ 27    + 32    + 27    + 58    + 32
```

4.
```
 624     537     384     275     108
+ 167   + 226   + 409   + 316   + 258
```

5.
```
 843     426     527     753     633
+ 127   + 236   + 169   + 237   + 148
```

6.
```
 363     147     531
+ 27    + 28    + 59
```

Subtraction with Regrouping

Solve the problems below.

1.
$$\begin{array}{r} \overset{2\ \ 1}{\cancel{3}6} \\ -\ 17 \\ \hline \mathbf{19} \end{array}$$
$$\begin{array}{r} 98 \\ -\ 19 \\ \hline \end{array}$$
$$\begin{array}{r} 28 \\ -\ 9 \\ \hline \end{array}$$
$$\begin{array}{r} 41 \\ -\ 15 \\ \hline \end{array}$$
$$\begin{array}{r} 13 \\ -\ 7 \\ \hline \end{array}$$

2.
$$\begin{array}{r} 72 \\ -\ 53 \\ \hline \end{array}$$
$$\begin{array}{r} 85 \\ -\ 27 \\ \hline \end{array}$$
$$\begin{array}{r} 43 \\ -\ 29 \\ \hline \end{array}$$
$$\begin{array}{r} 96 \\ -\ 37 \\ \hline \end{array}$$
$$\begin{array}{r} 64 \\ -\ 36 \\ \hline \end{array}$$

3.
$$\begin{array}{r} 47 \\ -\ 19 \\ \hline \end{array}$$
$$\begin{array}{r} 94 \\ -\ 26 \\ \hline \end{array}$$
$$\begin{array}{r} 75 \\ -\ 39 \\ \hline \end{array}$$
$$\begin{array}{r} 61 \\ -\ 22 \\ \hline \end{array}$$
$$\begin{array}{r} 33 \\ -\ 19 \\ \hline \end{array}$$

4.
$$\begin{array}{r} 371 \\ -\ 146 \\ \hline \end{array}$$
$$\begin{array}{r} 286 \\ -147 \\ \hline \end{array}$$
$$\begin{array}{r} 957 \\ -\ 329 \\ \hline \end{array}$$
$$\begin{array}{r} 465 \\ -\ 127 \\ \hline \end{array}$$
$$\begin{array}{r} 962 \\ -\ 344 \\ \hline \end{array}$$

5.
$$\begin{array}{r} 553 \\ -\ 129 \\ \hline \end{array}$$
$$\begin{array}{r} 476 \\ -\ 138 \\ \hline \end{array}$$
$$\begin{array}{r} 764 \\ -\ 335 \\ \hline \end{array}$$
$$\begin{array}{r} 676 \\ -\ 227 \\ \hline \end{array}$$
$$\begin{array}{r} 952 \\ -\ 344 \\ \hline \end{array}$$

6.
$$\begin{array}{r} 767 \\ -\ 18 \\ \hline \end{array}$$
$$\begin{array}{r} 350 \\ -\ 18 \\ \hline \end{array}$$
$$\begin{array}{r} 482 \\ -\ 35 \\ \hline \end{array}$$

2-Digit Addition and Subtraction: Word Problems

Solve the problems. Do your work in the box. Write your answer on the line.

1. Sam's basketball team scored 42 points. Nick's team only scored 28 points.

How many more points did Sam's team score than Nick's?

2. Jan had 57 seashells.

Her aunt sent her 26 more seashells for her collection.

How many seashells does Jan have now?

3. Nathan had 82 toy cars. He saved 15 special cars and gave the rest to his cousins.

How many cars did he give to his cousins?

4. A bike shop had 43 adult bikes and 38 children's bikes.

How many bikes did they have altogether?

5. Alexis sold 35 boxes of cookies. Amanda sold 28 boxes.

How many more boxes of cookies did Alexis sell than Amanda?

6. Phil had 34 books.

He lost 8 during his move.

How many books does he have left?

3-Digit Addition and Subtraction: Word Problems

Solve the problems. Do your work in the box. Write your answer on the line.

1. Roberto had 346 trading cards. He sold 188 cards at a trading card show.

How many cards does he have left?

_____

2. Mindy's class saved 121 soup labels. The rest of the school saved 699 labels.

How many labels does the school have altogether?

_____

3. Tran had 623 rocks in his collection. He found 17 more when he went hiking last week.

How many rocks does Tran have in all?

_____

4. The pet store had 435 fish for sale. They sold 178 fish last week.

How many fish do they have left?

_____

5. Devin has 728 coins in his collection. Kate has 649 coins in her collection.

How many more coins does Devin have than Kate?

_____

6. Kim has 321 marbles.

Kris has 399 marbles.

How many marbles do they have altogether?

_____

Write how many tens and ones are in each picture.
Then write the number that their combination makes.

1.

_**6**_ tens   _**2**_ ones

makes _**62**_

2.

____ tens   ____ ones

makes _____

3.

____ tens   ____ ones

makes _____

4.

____ tens   ____ ones

makes _____

5.

____ tens   ____ ones

makes _____

6.

____ tens   ____ ones

makes _____

Place Value: Hundreds, Tens, and Ones

Write how many hundreds, tens, and ones are in each picture. Then write the number that their combination makes.

1.

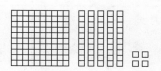

__1__ hundreds __5__ tens
__4__ ones = __154__

2.

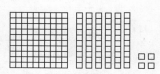

____ hundreds ____ tens
____ ones = _____

3.

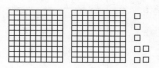

____ hundreds ____ tens
____ ones = _____

4.

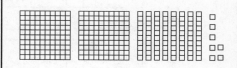

____ hundreds ____ tens
____ ones = _____

5.

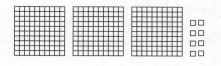

____ hundreds ____ tens
____ ones = _____

6.

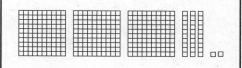

____ hundreds ____ tens
____ ones = _____

Place Value: Thousands, Hundreds, Tens, Ones

Write the value of each number.

		Ten Thousands	Thousands	Hundreds	Tens	Ones
1.	5,739	0	5	7	3	9
2.	14,650					
3.	81					
4.	40,736					
5.	1,475					
6.	55,837					
7.	86,902					
8.	4,560					
9.	31,048					
10.	111					
11.	79,277					
12.	93					
13.	99,999					
14.	5					

This is the tastiest looking 221 I've ever seen!

What place value do the circled numbers represent?

1. 3,④5 6   **hundreds**   2. 9 0,②8 6 _____

3. ⑦,3 9 4 _____   4. ④7,5 1 9 _____

5. ①6,3 2 1 _____   6. 3 8,1②7 _____

7. 2 5,0④7 _____   8. ⑧4,0 3 1 _____

9. 3 9,⑤8 6 _____   10. 7②,7 9 7 _____

11. 5 8,7 2⑨ _____   12. 5 9,3⑥8 _____

13. 4 0,3⑦0 _____   14. 3 0,5 8④ _____

15. ⑦2,5 3 2 _____   16. 8⑥,3 9 5 _____

17. 9⑥,4 1 1 _____   18. 3 9,⑤8 6 _____

19. 8 3,0⑨5 _____   20. 5⑩,8 5 4 _____

Place Value: Thousands, Hundreds, Tens, Ones

Write the number that means the same.

1. 30,000 + 1,000 + 500 + 30 + 3 =   **31,533**

2. 70,000 + 5,000 + 900 + 40 + 7 =   _____

3. 91,000 + 3,000 + 700 + 50 + 5 =   _____

4. 150,000 + 7,000 + 400 + 70 + 9 =   _____

5. 560,000 + 9,000 + 100 + 20 + 1 =   _____

6. 320,000 + 40,000 + 300 + 10 + 2 =   _____

7. 210,000 + 50,000 + 3,000 + 500 + 6 =   _____

8. 730,000 + 10,000 + 6,000 + 90 + 8 =   _____

9. 640,000 + 20,000 + 3,000 + 500 + 6 =   _____

10. 950,000 + 10,000 + 6,000 + 90 + 8 =   _____

11. 100,000 + 40,000 + 7,000 + 400 + 30 = _____

12. 620,000 + 70,000 + 1,000 + 300 + 50 + 6 = _____

Follow the numbers in order from greater to smaller.

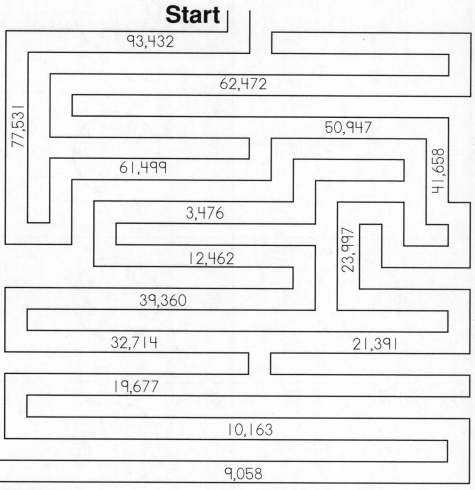

Start

93,432

62,472

77,531

50,947

61,499

41,658

3,476

23,997

12,462

39,360

32,714

21,391

19,677

10,163

9,058

Finish

Telling Time: Clock Hands

For problems 1 to 4, write the time shown on the clocks. For problems 5 to 8, draw hands on the clocks to show the time.

1. **6** : **50**	**2.** ___ : ___
3. ___ : ___	**4.** ___ : ___
5. 12:23	**6.** 10:25
7. 11:08	**8.** 4:47

Use the clocks to answer the questions.
All of the questions refer back to the original time shown on the clock.

1. What time does the clock show? ___**8:00**___

   What time would it be if it were 20 minutes earlier? _____

   What time will it be in 3 hours and 35 minutes? _____

   What time will it be in 65 minutes? _____

2. What time does the clock show? _____

   What time would it be if it were 48 minutes earlier? _____

   What time will it be in 5 hours and 22 minutes? _____

   What time will it be in 57 minutes? _____

3. What time does the clock show? _____

   What time would it be if it were 8 hours and 15 minutes earlier? _____

   What time will it be in 4 hours and 15 minutes? _____

   What time will it be in 75 minutes? _____

Math Grade 3—RBP3489

Solve the problems below. Use the illustrations to create sets. An example is done for you.

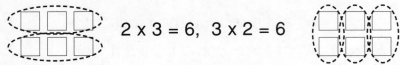 $2 \times 3 = 6, \quad 3 \times 2 = 6$

1. ____ x ____ = ____ , ____ x ____ = ____

2. ____ x ____ = ____ , ____ x ____ = ____

3. ____ x ____ = ____ , ____ x ____ = ____

4. ____ x ____ = ____ , ____ x ____ = ____

5. ____ x ____ = ____ , ____ x ____ = ____

6. ____ x ____ = ____ , ____ x ____ = ____

Multiplication: Sequence Counting

Relate these facts to complete the sequence.

1. $2 \times 4 = 8$ so $3 \times 4 = \underline{\textbf{12}}$ and $4 \times 4 = \underline{\textbf{16}}$

2. $5 \times 3 = 15$ so $6 \times 3 = \underline{\hspace{2em}}$ and $7 \times 3 = \underline{\hspace{2em}}$

3. $1 \times 6 = 6$ so $2 \times 6 = \underline{\hspace{2em}}$ and $3 \times 6 = \underline{\hspace{2em}}$

4. $2 \times 5 = 10$ so $3 \times 5 = \underline{\hspace{2em}}$ and $4 \times 5 = \underline{\hspace{2em}}$

5. $7 \times 3 = 21$ so $7 \times 4 = \underline{\hspace{2em}}$ and $7 \times 5 = \underline{\hspace{2em}}$

6. $3 \times 4 = 12$ so $4 \times 4 = \underline{\hspace{2em}}$ and $5 \times 4 = \underline{\hspace{2em}}$

7. $2 \times 9 = 18$ so $3 \times 9 = \underline{\hspace{2em}}$ and $4 \times 9 = \underline{\hspace{2em}}$

8. $4 \times 6 = 24$ so $5 \times 6 = \underline{\hspace{2em}}$ and $6 \times 6 = \underline{\hspace{2em}}$

9. $1 \times 8 = 8$ so $2 \times 8 = \underline{\hspace{2em}}$ and $3 \times 8 = \underline{\hspace{2em}}$

10. $2 \times 3 = 6$ so $3 \times 3 = \underline{\hspace{2em}}$ and $4 \times 3 = \underline{\hspace{2em}}$

11. $8 \times 3 = 24$ so $8 \times 4 = \underline{\hspace{2em}}$ and $8 \times 5 = \underline{\hspace{2em}}$

12. $9 \times 4 = 36$ so $9 \times 5 = \underline{\hspace{2em}}$ and $9 \times 6 = \underline{\hspace{2em}}$

Math Grade 3—RBP3489

Multiplication: Problem Solving

Solve each problem below.

1. 3 x 2 = **6**

   3 x 3 = _____

   3 x 4 = _____

   3 x 5 = _____

   3 x 6 = _____

   3 x 7 = _____

   3 x 8 = _____

   3 x 9 = _____

2. 4 x 2 = _____

   4 x 3 = _____

   4 x 4 = _____

   4 x 5 = _____

   4 x 6 = _____

   4 x 7 = _____

   4 x 8 = _____

   4 x 9 = _____

3. 5 x 2 = _____

   5 x 3 = _____

   5 x 4 = _____

   5 x 5 = _____

   5 x 6 = _____

   5 x 7 = _____

   5 x 8 = _____

   5 x 9 = _____

4. 6 x 2 = _____

   6 x 3 = _____

   6 x 4 = _____

   6 x 5 = _____

   6 x 6 = _____

   6 x 7 = _____

   6 x 8 = _____

   6 x 9 = _____

Multiplication: Problem Solving and Comparing

Use the >, <, or = signs to describe the relationship between the equations.

1. 2 x 6 $<$ 7 x 2   5 x 3 ◯ 4 x 4

2. 2 x 4 ◯ 6 x 1   9 x 4 ◯ 6 x 6

3. 7 x 5 ◯ 6 x 7   4 x 5 ◯ 5 x 3

4. 9 x 5 ◯ 10 x 4   6 x 7 ◯ 7 x 6

5. 8 x 4 ◯ 9 x 3   3 x 6 ◯ 4 x 5

6. 3 x 7 ◯ 5 x 5   10 x 5 ◯ 9 x 7

7. 6 x 0 ◯ 0 x 10   2 x 6 ◯ 3 x 4

8. 5 x 4 ◯ 5 x 3   9 x 1 ◯ 8 x 2

9. 47 x 1 ◯ 6 x 9   2 x 10 ◯ 5 x 4

10. 50 x 0 ◯ 5 x 10   5 x 9 ◯ 4 x 10

Multiplication: Word Problems

Solve the problems. Do your work in the box. Write your answer on the line.

1. Randy had 6 bags.

He put 9 marbles in each bag.

How many marbles did he have?

_____

2. Stan has 4 stacks of cards with 8 cards in each stack.

How many cards does he have?

_____

3. Jennifer jumped over 5 rocks. She jumped over each rock 9 times.

How many times did she jump?

_____

4. Zach runs 6 miles 5 days a week.

How many miles does he run in a week?

_____

5. The skaters skated in 7 groups with 4 in each group.

How many skaters were there in all?

_____

6. Eight children went for a hike. Each child carried a backpack with 6 bandages.

How many bandages did they have in all?

_____

Write the correct number in the blank.

1. 9 x __**1**__ = 9   3 x _____ = 21

2. 4 x _____ = 28   2 x _____ = 16

3. 5 x _____ = 40   7 x _____ = 42

4. _____ x 4 = 36   _____ x 6 = 54

5. _____ x 8 = 48   _____ x 3 = 15

6. 5 x 4 = _____   6 x 2 = _____

7. 0 x 5 = _____   _____ x 7 = 28

8. _____ x 2 = 14   8 x _____ = 56

9. 8 x _____ = 32   1 x _____ = 15

10. 10 x _____ = 0   _____ x 7 = 49

11. _____ x 5 = 50   9 x 1 = _____

12. 6 x _____ = 30   _____ x 10 = 100

Multiplication: Multiplication Wheels

Complete each wheel below by multiplying from the center out to the edge.

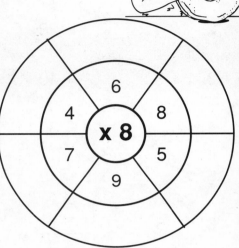

1.

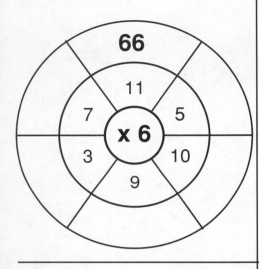

2.

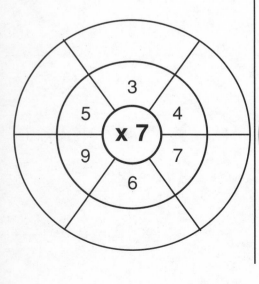

3.

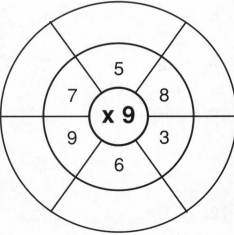

4.

©RBP Books

Division: Problem Solving

Solve each problem below.

1. How many 4s are there in 8? __2__ $8 \div 4 =$ __2__

2. How many 6s are there in 18? ____ $18 \div 6 =$ ____

3. How many 2s are there in 10? ____ $10 \div 2 =$ ____

4. How many 7s are there in 21? ____ $21 \div 7 =$ ____

5. How many 5s are there in 20? ____ $20 \div 5 =$ ____

6. How many 3s are there in 12? ____ $12 \div 3 =$ ____

7. How many 9s are there in 18? ____ $18 \div 9 =$ ____

8. How many 1s are there in 7? ____ $7 \div 1 =$ ____

9. How many 8s are there in 24? ____ $24 \div 8 =$ ____

10. How many 10s are there in 50? ____ $50 \div 10 =$ ____

Math Grade 3—RBP3489

Write the answer for each problem; then match it to the correct illustration.

1. $16 \div 8 =$ __2__

A.

2. $24 \div 4 =$ _____

B.

3. $21 \div 3 =$ _____

C.

4. $40 \div 8 =$ _____

D.

5. $32 \div 4 =$ _____

E.

6. $12 \div 4 =$ _____

F.

7. $36 \div 4 =$ _____

G.

Solve each problem below. Draw a graphic if it helps you find the answer.

1. $6 \div 2 =$ __**3**__

   $6 \div 3 =$ __**2**__

2. $12 \div 3 =$ _____

   $12 \div 4 =$ _____

3. $15 \div 5 =$ _____

   $15 \div 3 =$ _____

4. $10 \div 5 =$ _____

   $10 \div 2 =$ _____

5. $16 \div 2 =$ _____

   $16 \div 8 =$ _____

6. $20 \div 4 =$ _____

   $20 \div 5 =$ _____

7. $24 \div 6 =$ _____

   $24 \div 4 =$ _____

8. $28 \div 4 =$ _____

   $28 \div 7 =$ _____

9. $36 \div 9 =$ _____

   $36 \div 4 =$ _____

10. $16 \div 8 =$ _____

   $16 \div 2 =$ _____

11. $48 \div 6 =$ _____

   $48 \div 8 =$ _____

12. $54 \div 9 =$ _____

   $54 \div 6 =$ _____

Division: Problem Solving

Solve each problem below.

1. $5\overline{)40}$ **8**

2. $6\overline{)42}$

3. $3\overline{)27}$

4. $2\overline{)16}$

5. $7\overline{)49}$

6. $8\overline{)56}$

7. $4\overline{)16}$

8. $9\overline{)45}$

9. $10\overline{)90}$

10. $6\overline{)48}$

11. $7\overline{)56}$

12. $9\overline{)36}$

13. $5\overline{)30}$

14. $8\overline{)72}$

15. $9\overline{)63}$

16. $7\overline{)42}$

Multiplication and Division:
Fact Families

Solve each problem below.

1. 9 x 3 = __27__   3 x 9 = __27__   27 ÷ 9 = __3__

2. 4 x 7 = ____   7 x 4 = ____   28 ÷ 7 = ____

3. 2 x 8 = ____   8 x 2 = ____   16 ÷ 8 = ____

4. 5 x 6 = ____   6 x 5 = ____   30 ÷ 6 = ____

5. 6 x 9 = ____   9 x 6 = ____   54 ÷ 9 = ____

6. 8 x 7 = ____   7 x 8 = ____   56 ÷ 7 = ____

7. 45 ÷ 9 = ____   45 ÷ 5 = ____   9 x 5 = ____

8. 42 ÷ 6 = ____   42 ÷ 7 = ____   6 x 7 = ____

9. 63 ÷ 7 = ____   63 ÷ 9 = ____   9 x 7 = ____

10. 36 ÷ 9 = ____   36 ÷ 4 = ____   4 x 9 = ____

11. 48 ÷ 8 = ____   8 x 6 = ____   6 x 8 = ____

12. 72 ÷ 8 = ____   8 x 9 = ____   72 ÷ 9 = ____

13. 8 x 5 = ____   5 x 8 = ____   40 ÷ 8 = ____

14. 20 ÷ 4 = ____   4 x 5 = ____   20 ÷ 5 = ____

Solve each problem below.

1.
$$5 \times 4 = $$
20
$$4 \times 6$$
$$9 \times 7$$
$$7 \times 3$$
$$6 \times 5$$

2. $3 \overline{)27}$ $\qquad$ $7 \overline{)28}$ $\qquad$ $5 \overline{)40}$ $\qquad$ $8 \overline{)64}$

3. $81 \div 9 = \underline{}$ $\qquad$ $7 \times 5 = \underline{}$ $\qquad$ $28 \div 4 = \underline{}$

4. $6 \times 7 = \underline{}$ $\qquad$ $24 \div 6 = \underline{}$ $\qquad$ $18 \div 3 = \underline{}$

5. $8 \times 3 = \underline{}$ $\qquad$ $27 \div 9 = \underline{}$ $\qquad$ $20 \div 5 = \underline{}$

6. $10 \times 6 = \underline{}$ $\qquad$ $54 \div 6 = \underline{}$ $\qquad$ $8 \times 8 = \underline{}$

Multiplication: Mixed Problem Solving

Solve each problem below.

1. 3 x __9__ = 27   7 x _____ = 42   5 x _____ = 50

2. _____ x 7 = 49   9 x _____ = 81   4 x _____ = 28

3. _____ x 5 = 45   _____ x 4 = 12   _____ x 8 = 72

4. _____ x 8 = 64   6 x _____ = 48   _____ x 7 = 63

5.
32	32	10	42	89
x 4	x 3	x 6	x 2	x 0

6.
12	31	22	10	65
x 4	x 3	x 4	x 9	x 1

Money: Counting Coins

Add and write how much money there is in each box.

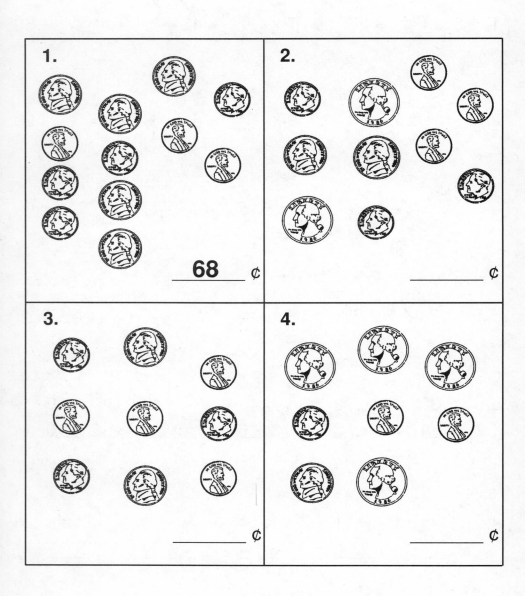

1. _____68_____ ¢

2. _____ ¢

3. _____ ¢

4. _____ ¢

Money: Counting Coins

Add and write how much money there is in each box.

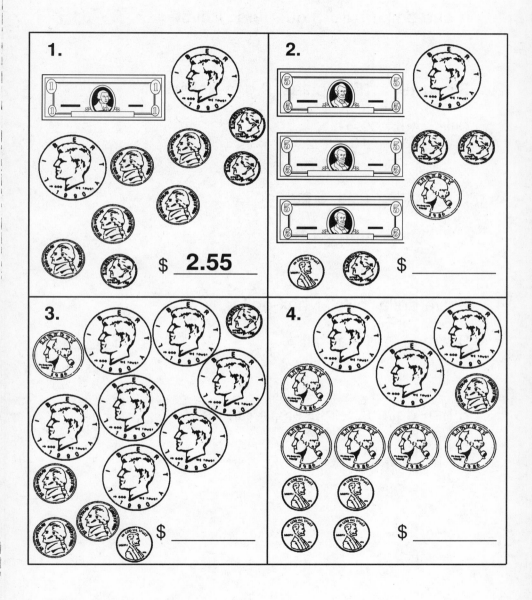

1. $ __2.55__

2. $ _____

3. $ _____

4. $ _____

Math Grade 3—RBP3489

Solve each problem below.

1. 4 one-dollar bills, 3 quarters, 1 dime = $ __4.85__

2. 5 quarters, 15 pennies, 9 one-dollar

    bills, 5 dimes = $____.____

3. 6 ten-dollar bills, 3 half-dollars,

    7 nickels, 1 quarter = $____.____

4. 6 five-dollar bills, 1 half-dollar,

    3 dimes, 1 dollar bill = $____.____

5. 8 half-dollars, 9 nickels, 4 dimes,

    3 five-dollar bills = $____.____

Wow!
Two quarters
are the same
as 50¢!

Adding and Subtracting Money with Regrouping

Solve each problem below.

1.
$$\begin{array}{r} \$7\overset{1}{3}\overset{1}{5}.41 \\ +\ 936.78 \\ \hline \mathbf{\$1,672.19} \end{array}$$
$$\begin{array}{r} \$368.90 \\ +\ 657.85 \\ \hline \end{array}$$
$$\begin{array}{r} \$643.30 \\ -\ 286.53 \\ \hline \end{array}$$

2.
$$\begin{array}{r} \$397.63 \\ +\ 583.97 \\ \hline \end{array}$$
$$\begin{array}{r} \$839.75 \\ -\ 659.75 \\ \hline \end{array}$$
$$\begin{array}{r} \$935.82 \\ -\ 758.97 \\ \hline \end{array}$$

3.
$$\begin{array}{r} \$9,964.35 \\ -\ 797.66 \\ \hline \end{array}$$
$$\begin{array}{r} \$9,759.38 \\ -\ 7,788.68 \\ \hline \end{array}$$
$$\begin{array}{r} \$6,045.36 \\ +\ 3,587.88 \\ \hline \end{array}$$

4.
$$\begin{array}{r} \$4,995.37 \\ +\ 9,327.83 \\ \hline \end{array}$$
$$\begin{array}{r} \$8,010.52 \\ -\ 7,936.67 \\ \hline \end{array}$$
$$\begin{array}{r} \$5,663.47 \\ +\ 5,459.53 \\ \hline \end{array}$$

5.
$$\begin{array}{r} \$8,983.31 \\ -\ 5,975.86 \\ \hline \end{array}$$
$$\begin{array}{r} \$5,143.18 \\ +\ 8,867.92 \\ \hline \end{array}$$
$$\begin{array}{r} \$5,930.77 \\ -\ 5,688.33 \\ \hline \end{array}$$

Money: Combinations

Use the money from page 43. In one bank put the greatest amount of money possible. In the other bank put the smallest amount possible. Follow this rule: Each bank must have 14 pieces of money, and each must have at least one of each type of coin or bill. Cross off bills or coins as you use them. Once crossed off you cannot use them again. You do not need to use all of the money shown.

$5 bills
$1 bills
quarters
dimes
nickels
pennies

total $ _____.

Least Amount

Greatest Amount

$5 bills
$1 bills
quarters
dimes
nickels
pennies

total $ _____.

For use with page 42.

Math Grade 3—RBP3489

Money: Word Problems

Solve the problems. Do your work in the box. Write your answer on the line.

1. Gina had $17.22. She earned $5.00 more for helping her mother.

How much did Gina have?

2. Matt had $18.77. He wanted to buy a CD for $14.50.

How much would he have left after he bought the CD?

3. Jon got $3.50 from his mother, $4.00 from his father, and $10.00 from his grandparents.

How much money did Jon get?

4. Len had $53.00. He was trying to earn enough money for a bike that cost $87.00.

How much more money does he need?

5. Dan earned $20.00 for mowing the neighbor's yard. He already had $12.00.

How much money does he have now?

6. Emma wanted to buy a science kit that cost $18.00. She only had $6.00.

How much more money does she need?

Write the equivalent fractions.

1. $\dfrac{1}{2} = \dfrac{2}{4}$ $\dfrac{3}{4} = \dfrac{}{8}$ $\dfrac{1}{3} = \dfrac{}{9}$

2. $\dfrac{3}{5} = \dfrac{}{15}$ $\dfrac{1}{2} = \dfrac{}{18}$ $\dfrac{1}{8} = \dfrac{}{24}$

3. $\dfrac{4}{9} = \dfrac{}{36}$ $\dfrac{5}{8} = \dfrac{}{40}$ $\dfrac{3}{7} = \dfrac{}{49}$

4. $\dfrac{4}{5} = \dfrac{}{45}$ $\dfrac{5}{7} = \dfrac{}{21}$ $\dfrac{7}{8} = \dfrac{}{72}$

Fractions: Addition and Subtraction

Solve each fraction problem below.

1. $\dfrac{2}{5} + \dfrac{1}{5} = \dfrac{3}{5}$ $\dfrac{3}{7} + \dfrac{2}{7} = $ —

2. $\dfrac{5}{12} + \dfrac{6}{12} = $ — $\dfrac{4}{9} + \dfrac{3}{9} = $ —

3. $\dfrac{13}{20} + \dfrac{6}{20} = $ — $\dfrac{5}{16} + \dfrac{8}{16} = $ —

4. $\dfrac{4}{9} - \dfrac{2}{9} = $ — $\dfrac{15}{20} - \dfrac{7}{20} = $ —

5. $\dfrac{7}{12} - \dfrac{3}{12} = $ — $\dfrac{16}{32} - \dfrac{9}{32} = $ —

6. $\dfrac{14}{24} - \dfrac{4}{24} = $ — $\dfrac{9}{14} - \dfrac{7}{14} = $ —

4-Digit Addition with Regrouping

Solve each problem below.

1.

$$\begin{array}{r} {\scriptstyle 1\ 1} \\ 3,261 \\ + 5,239 \\ \hline \mathbf{8,500} \end{array}$$

$$\begin{array}{r} 4,639 \\ + 2,073 \\ \hline \end{array}$$

$$\begin{array}{r} 7,216 \\ + 2,593 \\ \hline \end{array}$$

$$\begin{array}{r} 5,952 \\ + 3,128 \\ \hline \end{array}$$

2.

$$\begin{array}{r} 2,773 \\ + 3,535 \\ \hline \end{array}$$

$$\begin{array}{r} 9,076 \\ + 3,970 \\ \hline \end{array}$$

$$\begin{array}{r} 6,415 \\ + 1,765 \\ \hline \end{array}$$

$$\begin{array}{r} 4,701 \\ + 6,354 \\ \hline \end{array}$$

3.

$$\begin{array}{r} 3,257 \\ + 4,809 \\ \hline \end{array}$$

$$\begin{array}{r} 9,935 \\ + 1,260 \\ \hline \end{array}$$

$$\begin{array}{r} 1,224 \\ + 8,967 \\ \hline \end{array}$$

$$\begin{array}{r} 6,597 \\ + 3,212 \\ \hline \end{array}$$

4.

$$\begin{array}{r} 7,309 \\ + 4,597 \\ \hline \end{array}$$

$$\begin{array}{r} 3,295 \\ + 4,305 \\ \hline \end{array}$$

$$\begin{array}{r} 5,716 \\ + 1,708 \\ \hline \end{array}$$

$$\begin{array}{r} 6,907 \\ + 4,132 \\ \hline \end{array}$$

5.

$$\begin{array}{r} 1,943 \\ + 3,065 \\ \hline \end{array}$$

$$\begin{array}{r} 2,967 \\ + 7,120 \\ \hline \end{array}$$

$$\begin{array}{r} 3,846 \\ + 2,195 \\ \hline \end{array}$$

$$\begin{array}{r} 6,381 \\ + 5,436 \\ \hline \end{array}$$

Subtraction with Regrouping

Solve each problem below.

1. $\overset{8\ \ 16\ 1}{\cancel{9},3\cancel{7}5}$ 2,772   3,943   5,814
    − 4,969   − 1,476   − 1,876   − 2,867
    4,406

2. 7,403   9,800   5,639   7,860
    − 2,675   − 3,765   − 1,879   − 1,895

3. 8,207   9,730   7,796   3,905
    − 4,648   − 4,698   − 2,994   − 1,847

4. 27,436   56,943   33,845   80,560
    − 7,527   − 37,880   − 11,966   − 26,483

5. 78,571   50,965   46,739   75,430
    − 37,875   − 15,879   − 36,465   − 29,767

4-Digit Addition and Subtraction: Word Problems

Solve the problems. Do your work in the box. Write your answer on the line.

1. 2,479 people went to the concert on Friday night.
3,210 people went to the concert on Saturday night.

a. How many people went to the concert?

_____

b. How many more people attended on Saturday night than Friday?

_____

2. 1,324 students graduated from East High School.
1,129 students graduated from West High School.

a. How many students graduated from the two high schools?

_____

b. How many more students graduated from East than West?

_____

3. 8,721 people live in Littletown.
7,820 people live in Smalltown.

a. How many more people live in Littletown than in Smalltown?

_____

b. How many people live in the two towns?

_____

49

Look at the geometric solids. Each side is called a face. Write the number of faces each block has.

1.

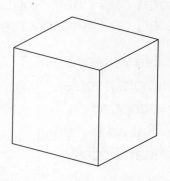

cube

_____ ☐ faces

2.

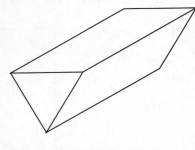

triangular prism

_____ △ faces

_____ ☐ faces

3.

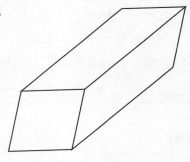

square prism

_____ ☐ faces

_____ ☐ faces

4.

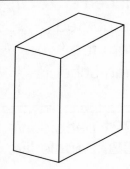

rectangular prism

_____ ☐ faces

_____ ☐ faces

50

Fractions and Decimals: Problem Solving

Fill in the blanks with the number of tenths, the fraction, and a decimal for each problem.

1.

_____**1**_____ tenth
_____**1/10**_____ fraction
_____**.1**_____ decimal

2.

_____ tenths
_____ fraction
_____ decimal

3.

_____ tenths
_____ fraction
_____ decimal

4.

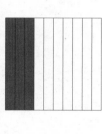

_____ tenths
_____ fraction
_____ decimal

5.

_____ tenths
_____ fraction
_____ decimal

6.

_____ tenths
_____ fraction
_____ decimal

Fractions and Decimals: Problem Solving

Shade in the correct number of squares in each box to equal the decimal.

1.

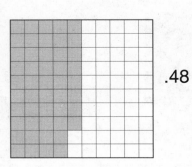

.48

2.

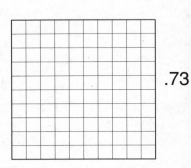

.73

3.

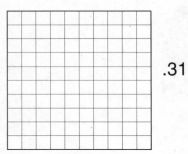

.31

4.

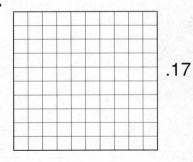

.17

5.

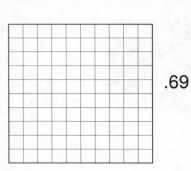

.69

6.

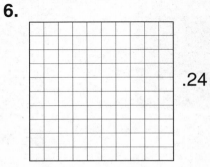

.24

Multiplication with Regrouping

Solve each problem below.

1.

$$\begin{array}{r} \overset{1}{26} \\ \times\ 2 \\ \hline \mathbf{52} \end{array}$$
$$\begin{array}{r} 31 \\ \times\ 2 \\ \hline \end{array}$$
$$\begin{array}{r} 47 \\ \times\ 2 \\ \hline \end{array}$$
$$\begin{array}{r} 81 \\ \times\ 2 \\ \hline \end{array}$$
$$\begin{array}{r} 73 \\ \times\ 2 \\ \hline \end{array}$$

2.

$$\begin{array}{r} 17 \\ \times\ 3 \\ \hline \end{array}$$
$$\begin{array}{r} 23 \\ \times\ 3 \\ \hline \end{array}$$
$$\begin{array}{r} 91 \\ \times\ 3 \\ \hline \end{array}$$
$$\begin{array}{r} 72 \\ \times\ 3 \\ \hline \end{array}$$
$$\begin{array}{r} 84 \\ \times\ 3 \\ \hline \end{array}$$

3.

$$\begin{array}{r} 54 \\ \times\ 4 \\ \hline \end{array}$$
$$\begin{array}{r} 72 \\ \times\ 4 \\ \hline \end{array}$$
$$\begin{array}{r} 95 \\ \times\ 4 \\ \hline \end{array}$$
$$\begin{array}{r} 42 \\ \times\ 4 \\ \hline \end{array}$$
$$\begin{array}{r} 57 \\ \times\ 4 \\ \hline \end{array}$$

4.

$$\begin{array}{r} 48 \\ \times\ 5 \\ \hline \end{array}$$
$$\begin{array}{r} 33 \\ \times\ 5 \\ \hline \end{array}$$
$$\begin{array}{r} 90 \\ \times\ 5 \\ \hline \end{array}$$
$$\begin{array}{r} 72 \\ \times\ 5 \\ \hline \end{array}$$
$$\begin{array}{r} 86 \\ \times\ 5 \\ \hline \end{array}$$

5.

$$\begin{array}{r} 16 \\ \times\ 6 \\ \hline \end{array}$$
$$\begin{array}{r} 97 \\ \times\ 6 \\ \hline \end{array}$$
$$\begin{array}{r} 41 \\ \times\ 6 \\ \hline \end{array}$$
$$\begin{array}{r} 82 \\ \times\ 6 \\ \hline \end{array}$$
$$\begin{array}{r} 77 \\ \times\ 6 \\ \hline \end{array}$$

6.

$$\begin{array}{r} 54 \\ \times\ 2 \\ \hline \end{array}$$
$$\begin{array}{r} 46 \\ \times\ 3 \\ \hline \end{array}$$
$$\begin{array}{r} 39 \\ \times\ 4 \\ \hline \end{array}$$
$$\begin{array}{r} 65 \\ \times\ 5 \\ \hline \end{array}$$
$$\begin{array}{r} 65 \\ \times\ 6 \\ \hline \end{array}$$

Math Grade 3—RBP3489

Solve each problem below.

1.
$$\begin{array}{r} {}^{4}17 \\ \times\ 7 \\ \hline \mathbf{119} \end{array}$$
$$\begin{array}{r} 19 \\ \times\ 7 \\ \hline \end{array}$$
$$\begin{array}{r} 23 \\ \times\ 7 \\ \hline \end{array}$$
$$\begin{array}{r} 46 \\ \times\ 7 \\ \hline \end{array}$$
$$\begin{array}{r} 37 \\ \times\ 7 \\ \hline \end{array}$$

2.
$$\begin{array}{r} 63 \\ \times\ 8 \\ \hline \end{array}$$
$$\begin{array}{r} 21 \\ \times\ 8 \\ \hline \end{array}$$
$$\begin{array}{r} 92 \\ \times\ 8 \\ \hline \end{array}$$
$$\begin{array}{r} 83 \\ \times\ 8 \\ \hline \end{array}$$
$$\begin{array}{r} 47 \\ \times\ 8 \\ \hline \end{array}$$

3.
$$\begin{array}{r} 84 \\ \times\ 9 \\ \hline \end{array}$$
$$\begin{array}{r} 27 \\ \times\ 9 \\ \hline \end{array}$$
$$\begin{array}{r} 90 \\ \times\ 9 \\ \hline \end{array}$$
$$\begin{array}{r} 57 \\ \times\ 9 \\ \hline \end{array}$$
$$\begin{array}{r} 75 \\ \times\ 9 \\ \hline \end{array}$$

4.
$$\begin{array}{r} 72 \\ \times\ 10 \\ \hline \end{array}$$
$$\begin{array}{r} 97 \\ \times\ 10 \\ \hline \end{array}$$
$$\begin{array}{r} 36 \\ \times\ 10 \\ \hline \end{array}$$
$$\begin{array}{r} 44 \\ \times\ 10 \\ \hline \end{array}$$
$$\begin{array}{r} 85 \\ \times\ 10 \\ \hline \end{array}$$

5.
$$\begin{array}{r} 59 \\ \times\ 7 \\ \hline \end{array}$$
$$\begin{array}{r} 76 \\ \times\ 8 \\ \hline \end{array}$$
$$\begin{array}{r} 66 \\ \times\ 9 \\ \hline \end{array}$$
$$\begin{array}{r} 59 \\ \times\ 10 \\ \hline \end{array}$$
$$\begin{array}{r} 73 \\ \times\ 8 \\ \hline \end{array}$$

2-Digit Multiplication: Word Problems

Solve the problems. Do your work in the box. Write your answer on the line.

1. Jim brought cookies to school to share. He wants each student to get 3.

There are 29 students. How many cookies does he need?

_____

2. Kara has 7 feet of ribbon. She knows there are 12 inches in each foot.

How many inches of ribbon does she have?

_____

3. Tina rode her bike 17 miles each day for 6 days.

How many miles did Tina ride?

_____

4. Jack read 7 books.

Each book had 48 pages.

How many pages did Jack read?

_____

5. Marissa has 5 trading card books. Each book has 50 cards in it.

How many trading cards does Marissa have?

_____

6. Juan put his stamp collection into 4 boxes. He put 73 stamps in each box.

How many stamps does he have?

_____

Multiplication Practice

Solve each problem below.

1. $5 \times 3 \times 2 = $ __**30**__ $2 \times 6 \times 1 = $ ____ $4 \times 10 \times 1 = $ ___

2. $7 \times 2 \times 2 = $ ____ $4 \times 5 \times 2 = $ ____ $3 \times 1 \times 6 = $ ___

3. $6 \times 2 \times 3 = $ ____ $3 \times 5 \times 2 = $ ____ $4 \times 3 \times 3 = $ ___

4. $10 \times 2 \times 3 = $ ____ $3 \times 2 \times 10 = $ ____ $5 \times 2 \times 10 = $ ___

5. $4 \times 2 \times 5 = $ ____ $6 \times 3 \times 3 = $ ____ $14 \times 3 \times 0 = $ ___

6. $1 \times 6 \times 9 = $ ____ $2 \times 5 \times 0 = $ ____ $1 \times 7 \times 8 = $ ___

Multiplication Practice

Solve each problem below.

1.
$$
\begin{array}{r} {}^{2}63 \\ \times\ 7 \\ \hline \mathbf{441} \end{array}
$$
$$
\begin{array}{r} 65 \\ \times\ 3 \\ \hline \end{array}
$$
$$
\begin{array}{r} 69 \\ \times\ 5 \\ \hline \end{array}
$$
$$
\begin{array}{r} 64 \\ \times\ 9 \\ \hline \end{array}
$$
$$
\begin{array}{r} 67 \\ \times\ 7 \\ \hline \end{array}
$$

2.
$$
\begin{array}{r} 77 \\ \times\ 5 \\ \hline \end{array}
$$
$$
\begin{array}{r} 71 \\ \times\ 9 \\ \hline \end{array}
$$
$$
\begin{array}{r} 70 \\ \times\ 6 \\ \hline \end{array}
$$
$$
\begin{array}{r} 75 \\ \times\ 8 \\ \hline \end{array}
$$
$$
\begin{array}{r} 76 \\ \times\ 4 \\ \hline \end{array}
$$

3.
$$
\begin{array}{r} 82 \\ \times\ 7 \\ \hline \end{array}
$$
$$
\begin{array}{r} 85 \\ \times\ 6 \\ \hline \end{array}
$$
$$
\begin{array}{r} 89 \\ \times\ 3 \\ \hline \end{array}
$$
$$
\begin{array}{r} 83 \\ \times\ 9 \\ \hline \end{array}
$$
$$
\begin{array}{r} 88 \\ \times\ 5 \\ \hline \end{array}
$$

4.
$$
\begin{array}{r} 90 \\ \times\ 7 \\ \hline \end{array}
$$
$$
\begin{array}{r} 92 \\ \times\ 9 \\ \hline \end{array}
$$
$$
\begin{array}{r} 96 \\ \times\ 8 \\ \hline \end{array}
$$
$$
\begin{array}{r} 95 \\ \times\ 6 \\ \hline \end{array}
$$
$$
\begin{array}{r} 99 \\ \times\ 4 \\ \hline \end{array}
$$

5.
$$
\begin{array}{r} 62 \\ \times\ 8 \\ \hline \end{array}
$$
$$
\begin{array}{r} 79 \\ \times\ 7 \\ \hline \end{array}
$$
$$
\begin{array}{r} 86 \\ \times\ 7 \\ \hline \end{array}
$$
$$
\begin{array}{r} 94 \\ \times\ 5 \\ \hline \end{array}
$$
$$
\begin{array}{r} 39 \\ \times\ 8 \\ \hline \end{array}
$$

Math Grade 3—RBP3489

Multiplication Practice

Solve each problem below.

Whoa! I'm multiplying!

1. $^{3}45 \times 7 =$ **315** $39 \times 7 =$ _____ $26 \times 9 =$ ___

2. $53 \times 4 =$ _____ $27 \times 3 =$ _____ $38 \times 4 =$ ___

3. $13 \times 8 =$ _____ $54 \times 3 =$ _____ $99 \times 5 =$ ___

4. $28 \times 3 =$ _____ $57 \times 8 =$ _____ $69 \times 4 =$ ___

5. $17 \times 5 =$ _____ $29 \times 6 =$ _____ $83 \times 4 =$ ___

6. $5 \times 2 \times 6 =$ _____ $3 \times 5 \times 9 =$ _____ $7 \times 4 \times 5 =$ ___

7. $6 \times 5 \times 4 =$ _____ $9 \times 3 \times 2 =$ _____ $8 \times 5 \times 7 =$ ___

©RBP Books

Math Investigations

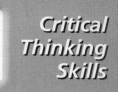

Count by 2s and 10s.
How many do you have in your house?

1. Toes

Did you count by 2 or 10?____
How many did you count?____

2. Eyes

Did you count by 2 or 10?____
How many did you count?____

3. Ears

Did you count by 2 or 10?____
How many did you count?____

4. Fingers

Did you count by 2 or 10?____
How many did you count?____

5. Sock with Shoes

Did you count by 2 or 10?____
How many did you count?____

6. Knees

Did you count by 2 or 10?____
How many did you count?____

7. Elbows

Did you count by 2 or 10?____
How many did you count?____

8. Feet

Did you count by 2 or 10?____
How many did you count?____

Math Investigations

What are the next three numbers in each pattern? Complete the rule.

1.   20   30   40   ___   ___   ___

RULE: Increase the number in the __**tens**__ place by __**1**__.

2.   300   400   500   ___   ___   ___

RULE: Increase the number in the _____ place by _____.

3.   5   10   15   ___   ___   ___

RULE: Increase the number in the _____ place by _____.

4.   55   65   75   ___   ___   ___

RULE: Increase the number in the _____ place by _____.

5.   700   600   500   ___   ___   ___

RULE: Decrease the number in the _____ place by _____.

6.   9   8   7   ___   ___   ___

RULE: Decrease the number in the _____ place by _____.

Math Investigations

Animals have different life spans. *Life span* means the number of years something lives. The life spans of some animals are shown in the bar graph.

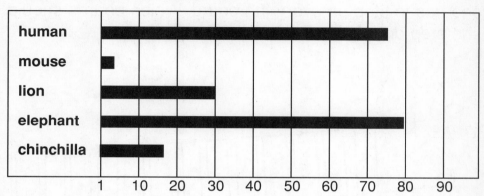

1. Which animal lives the least number of years? Why do you think that?

_____

_____

2. Which animal lives the longest? How do you know that?

_____

_____

3. Which animal is likely to live as long as you do? Explain.

_____

_____

4. What is the difference in life span between the…

mouse and elephant_____

lion and mouse_____

human and chinchilla_____

Math Investigations

A hiker is trying to hike across the Grand Canyon. There is an old bridge that crosses the Colorado River near the bottom of the canyon. To get across the bridge the hiker realizes that she has to step on every 4th board. Which boards should she step on to get across?

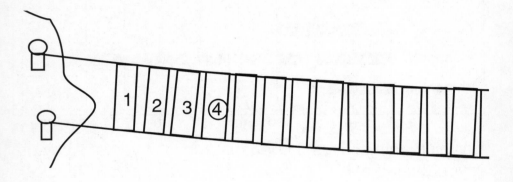

If each step is 1 foot wide, and if the Colorado River is 145 feet wide, what number will the last step land on? Write the numbers below in order.

4									

Math Investigations

Here are two 50-square grids. The first lists the even numbers from 2 to 50. The second lists the odd numbers from 1 to 49. Some numbers are missing.
Fill in the missing numbers.

Even

	2		4		6		8		10
	12		14						
							28		30
	32								
					46		48		50

Odd

1		3		5		7		9	
11		13							
						27			
31									
				45		47		49	

What patterns can you see in the charts?

Math Investigations

Use the numbers on the houses below to write the missing three-digit numbers.

1 4 8

Numbers greater than 400
__481__   __418__   __814__   __841__

Numbers less than 500

___   ___   ___   ___

Numbers greater than 800

___   ___

Numbers less than 300

___   ___

Numbers greater than 160 and less than 500

___   ___   ___

Numbers greater than 450 and less than 820

___   ___

3 5 7

Numbers greater than 500
__573__   ___   ___   ___

Numbers less than 600

___   ___   ___   ___

Numbers greater than 700

___   ___

Numbers less than 400

___   ___

Numbers greater than 350 and less than 550

___   ___   ___

Numbers greater than 550 and less than 750

___   ___

Math Investigations

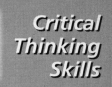

The table shows how many eggs different insects and spiders lay.

Insect or Spider	Number of Eggs
Water Spider	About 50–100
Cabbage Butterfly	About 300
Praying Mantis	About 10–400
Ladybug	About 3–300

1. Which insects or spiders can lay less than 150 eggs?

_____

_____

2. What is the least number of eggs the water spider lays?

_____

3. What is the greatest number of eggs a ladybug can lay?

_____

4. Which insects can lay more than 300 eggs?

_____

_____

5. If each insect and spider laid all the eggs possible, how many eggs would they lay altogether? Show your work below.

Math Investigations

The depth at which each of these ocean animals usually lives is written below.

Whale: 500 feet
Jellyfish: 10 feet
Shark: 250 feet
Octopus: 5,000 feet
Sponge: 300 feet
Crab: 1 foot
Lobster: 5 feet
Sea Bass: 100 feet

Pretend you dove from a boat. Write in order the sea animals you would see as you dove to 5,000 feet.

_____
_____
_____
_____

What animal would you see last? _____

Why do you think different sea animals live at different levels in the sea?

The Big Race

Matt and Denise are going to race. Since Denise is older, she is letting Matt have a head start. Based on the information below, who will win the race?

Denise runs 10 ft. per second.
Matt runs 5 ft. per second.
Denise is 40 ft. from Matt.
Matt is 20 ft. from the finish line.

Who will win? _____

Factoid!
A cheetah can run more than 70 miles per hour!

Happy Birthday!

Lori is twice as old as Allie. In five years' time, Allie will be as old as Lori is now.

How old is Lori? _____

How old is Allie? _____

FACTOID!

The human body has 206 bones!

© RBP Books

Time Teaser

Draw a straight line to split the clock face below in half so that the sum of the numbers on one side of the line will equal the sum of the numbers on the other side.

Number Puzzle—Part 1

Fill in the crossword puzzle on the following page using the clues provided below.

Across

1. $2,000 + 500 + 30 + 5$
2. $550,000 + 420 + 30$
3. $7,800 - 2,000 - 400 - 50$
4. $70,000 + 6,000 + 470 + 2$
5. $19,165 + 120 + 5$
6. $6,985 - 1,550 - 3,000 - 35$
7. $49,915 - 22,000 - 610$
8. $5,000 + 32,000 + 400 + 96$

Down

9. $30,000 + 8,000 + 200 + 25$
10. $15,448 - 7,200 - 7,100 - 2$
11. $50,475 - 15,000 - 200 - 50$
12. $50,000 + 22,000 + 395 + 5$
13. $55,000 + 275 + 25 + 30$
14. $13,565 - 9,000 - 300 - 45$
15. $82,690 - 40,000 - 1,000 - 420$
16. $77,200 - 5,000 - 100 - 10$

Number Puzzle—Part 2

This should be a piece of cake for a genius like you!

Math Grade 3—RBP3489

Critical Thinking Skills

Fractions

Write the fraction for the shaded part of each shape.

1.  $\frac{2}{8}$ or $\frac{1}{4}$

2.  ___ or ___

3. ___ or ___

4. ___ or ___

Shade in the shapes to make equivalent fractions (fractions that equal the same amount) and write the equal fraction.

5. $\frac{1}{2}$ or $\frac{2}{4}$ = _____

6. $\frac{2}{3}$ or $\frac{4}{6}$ = _____

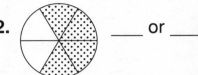

Factoid!
The origin of the word *school* is traced back to the Greek word *schole*, meaning "leisure."

Critical Thinking Skills

Fractions

Write the fraction for the shaded part of each shape.

1.  $\frac{2}{8}$ or $\frac{1}{4}$

2.  ___ or ___

3. ___ or ___

4.   ___ or ___

Shade in the shapes to make equivalent fractions (fractions that equal the same amount) and write the equal fraction.

5. $\frac{1}{2}$ or $\frac{2}{4}$ = _____

6. 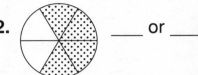 $\frac{2}{3}$ or $\frac{4}{6}$ = _____

Factoid!
The origin of the word *school* is traced back to the Greek word *schole*, meaning "leisure."

www.summerbridgeactivities.com

72

©RBP Books

A Penny Saved

Matt has saved his coins all summer long in his piggy bank. Matt has pennies, nickels, dimes, and quarters. He has the same number of each coin. Matt has $2.46 in his piggy bank. How many pennies, nickels, dimes, and quarters does he have?

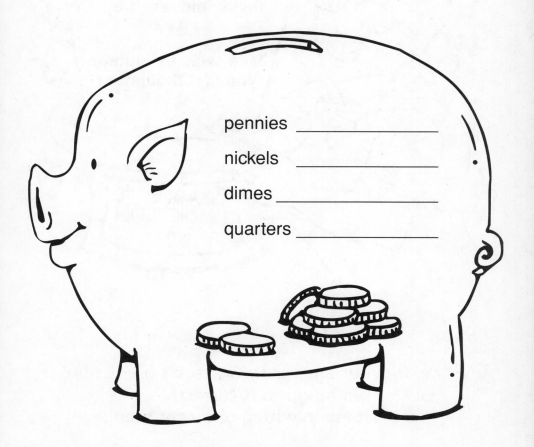

pennies _____

nickels _____

dimes _____

quarters _____

Number Magic

Think of a number and then do the following things to it.

Take away 2.
Multiply the result by 3.
Add 12.
Divide the result by 3.
Add 5.

Take away the number you first thought of.

GRAYSON'S PREDICTION
7

Compare your answer to Grayson's prediction.
Did he guess it correctly?
Now try it again with a different number.

Answer Pages

Page 3
1. 4, 5, 10   **2.** 7, 10, 9
3. 12, 16, 9   **4.** 5, 6, 17
5. 13, 0, 12   **6.** 8, 12, 11
7. 15, 9, 17   **8.** 7, 7, 12
9. 4, 9, 14   **10.** 14, 13, 8
11. 15, 7, 7   **12.** 18, 13, 5
13. 16, 12, 12   **14.** 9, 11, 3
15. 2, 7, 14   **16.** 10, 13, 6

Page 4
1. 9, 10, 15, 15, 16   **2.** 13, 14, 9, 14, 9
3. 16, 18, 15, 13, 5   **4.** 14, 8, 16, 7, 9
5. 18, 13, 17, 12, 15   **6.** 13, 4, 5, 18, 6

Page 5
1. 13, 13, 11, 15, 17
2. 13, 15, 15, 18, 18
3. 16, 17, 17, 18, 18

Page 6

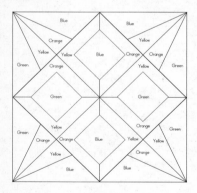

Page 7
1. 65, 89, 78, 58, 85
2. 97, 99, 59, 89, 89
3. 89, 59, 87, 99, 96
4. 788, 985, 867, 877, 798
5. 786, 786, 879, 769, 888

Page 8
1. 54, 40, 22, 65, 61
2. 24, 23, 51, 50, 32
3. 24, 24, 22, 10, 40
4. 272, 141, 150
5. 63, 137, 462
6. 315, 923, 415

Page 9

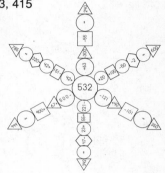

Page 10
1. 51, 92, 83, 86, 64
2. 94, 100, 92, 92, 103
3. 93, 111, 70, 114, 130
4. 791, 763, 793, 591, 366
5. 970, 662, 696, 990, 781
6. 390, 175, 590

Page 11
1. 19, 79, 19, 26, 6
2. 19, 58, 14, 59, 28
3. 28, 68, 36, 39, 14
4. 225, 139, 628, 338, 618
5. 424, 338, 429, 449, 608
6. 749, 332, 447

Page 12
1. 42-28=14 – Sam's team scored 14 more points.
2. 57+26=83 – Jan has 83 shells.
3. 82-15=67 – Nathan gave 67 cars to his cousins.
4. 43+38=81 – The bike shop has 81 bikes.
5. 35-28=7 – Alexis sold 7 more boxes.
6. 34-8=26 – Phil has 26 books left.

Answer Pages

Page 13

1. 346-188=158 – Roberto has 158 cards left.
2. 121+699=820 – The school has 820 labels.
3. 623+17=640 – Tran has 640 rocks.
4. 435-178=257 – The pet store has 257 fish left.
5. 728-649=79 – Devin has 79 more coins than Kate.
6. 321+399=720 – They have 720 marbles altogether.

Page 14

1. 6 tens, 2 ones=62
2. 4 tens, 9 ones=49
3. 1 tens, 9 ones=19
4. 2 ten, 9 ones=29
5. 7 tens, 4 ones=74
6. 3 tens, 8 ones=38

Page 15

1. 1 hundred, 5 tens, 4 ones=154
2. 1 hundred, 6 tens, 4 ones=164
3. 2 hundreds, 0 tens, 7 ones=207
4. 2 hundreds, 8 tens, 7 ones=287
5. 3 hundreds, 0 tens, 8 ones=308
6. 3 hundreds, 3 tens, 2 ones=332

Page 16

1. 0, 5, 7, 3, 9
2. 1, 4, 6, 5, 0
3. 0, 0, 0, 8, 1
4. 4, 0, 7, 3, 6
5. 0, 1, 4, 7, 5
6. 5, 5, 8, 3, 7
7. 8, 6, 9, 0, 2
8. 0, 4, 5, 6, 0
9. 3, 1, 0, 4, 8
10. 0, 0, 1, 1, 1
11. 7, 9, 2, 7, 7
12. 0, 0, 0, 9, 3
13. 9, 9, 9, 9, 9
14. 0, 0, 0, 0, 5

Page 17

1. hundreds
2. hundreds
3. thousands
4. ten thousands
5. ten thousands
6. tens
7. tens
8. ten thousands
9. hundreds
10. thousands
11. ones
12. tens

13. tens
14. ones
15. ten thousands
16. thousands
17. thousands
18. hundreds
19. tens
20. thousands

Page 18

1. 31,533
2. 75,947
3. 94,755
4. 157,479
5. 569,121
6. 360,312
7. 263,506
8. 746,098
9. 663,506
10. 966,098
11. 147,430
12. 691,356

Page 19

1. 93,432; 77,531; 61,499; 50,947; 41,658; 23,997; 21,391; 19,677; 10,163; 9,058

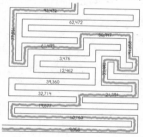

Page 20

1. 6:50
2. 6:00
3. 1:30
4. 3:55
5.
6.
7.
8.

Page 21

1. 8:00, 7:40, 11:35, 9:05
2. 1:33, 12:45, 6:55, 2:30
3. 10:45, 2:30, 3:00, 12:00

Page 22

1. 2x4=8, 4x2=8
2. 2x6=12, 6x2=12;
3. 3x4=12, 4x3=12
4. 3x5=15, 5x3=15;
5. 2x5=10, 5x2=10
6. 4x5=20, 5x4=20.

76

Answer Pages

Page 23
1. 12, 16   **2.** 18, 21   **3.** 12, 18   **4.** 15, 20
5. 28, 35   **6.** 16, 20   **7.** 27, 36   **8.** 30, 36
9. 16, 24   **10.** 9, 12   **11.** 32, 40   **12.** 45, 54

Page 24
1. 6, 9, 12, 15, 18, 21 24, 27
2. 8, 12, 16, 20, 24, 28, 32, 36
3. 10, 15, 20, 25, 30, 35, 40 45
4. 12, 18, 24, 30, 36, 42, 48, 54

Page 25
1. <, <   **2.** >, =   **3.** <, >   **4.** >, =
5. >, <   **6.** <, <   **7.** =, =   **8.** >, <
9. <, =   **10.** <, >

Page 26
1. 6x9=54 – Randy has 54 marbles.
2. 4x8=32 – Stan has 32 cards.
3. 5x9=45 – Jennifer jumped 45 times.
4. 6x5=30 – Zach ran 30 miles each week.
5. 7x4=28 – There were 28 skaters.
6. 8x6=48 – They had 48 bandages.

Page 27
1. 1, 7   **2.** 7, 8   **3.** 8, 6   **4.** 9, 9
5. 6, 5   **6.** 20, 12   **7.** 0, 4   **8.** 7, 7
9. 4, 15   **10.** 0, 7   **11.** 10, 9   **12.** 5, 10

Page 28
Answers start at top and move clockwise.
1. 66, 30, 60, 54, 18, 42
2. 48, 64, 40, 72, 56, 32
3. 21, 28, 49, 42, 63, 35
4. 45, 72, 27, 54, 81, 63

Page 29
1. 2, 2   **2.** 3, 3   **3.** 5, 5   **4.** 3, 3
5. 4, 4   **6.** 4, 4   **7.** 2, 2   **8.** 7, 7
9. 3, 3   **10.** 5, 5

Page 30
1. 2, B is the match.   **2.** 6, C is the match.
3. 7, A is the match.   **4.** 5, F is the match.
5. 8, G is the match.   **6.** 3, D is the match.
7. 9, E is the match.

Page 31
1. 3, 2   **2.** 4, 3   **3.** 3, 5   **4.** 2, 5
5. 8, 2   **6.** 5, 4   **7.** 4, 6   **8.** 7, 4
9. 4, 9   **10.** 2, 8   **11.** 8, 6   **12.** 6, 9

Page 32
1. 8   **2.** 7   **3.** 9   **4.** 8
5. 7   **6.** 7   **7.** 4   **8.** 5
9. 9   **10.** 8   **11.** 8   **12.** 4
13. 6   **14.** 9   **15.** 7   **16.** 6

Page 33
1. 12÷2=6   There will be 6 goldfish in each tank.
2. 8÷2=4   Deb will wear 4 bracelets on each wrist.
3. 16÷4=4   The team scored 4 points each quarter.
4. 15÷3=5   Nick has 5 trophies on each shelf.
5. 18÷6=3   Jan sewed 3 buttons on each pocket.
6. 35÷7=5   Kelly will need 5 pages.

Page 34
1. 5, 7, 9, 2, 4, 6, 8   **2.** 4, 6, 8, 10, 3, 5, 7
3. 9, 3, 8, 4, 10, 7, 6   **4.** 4, 6, 10, 8, 3, 5, 7

Page 35
1. 27, 27, 3   **2.** 28, 28, 4   **3.** 16, 16, 2
4. 30, 30, 5   **5.** 54, 54, 6   **6.** 56, 56, 8
7. 5, 9, 45   **8.** 7, 6, 42   **9.** 9, 7, 63
10. 4, 9, 36   **11.** 6, 48, 48   **12.** 9, 72, 8
13. 40, 40, 5   **14.** 5, 20, 4

Page 36
1. 20, 24, 63, 21, 30   **2.** 9, 4, 8, 8
3. 9, 35, 7   **4.** 42, 4, 6   **5.** 24, 3, 4
6. 60, 9, 64

Answer Pages

Page 37
1. 9, 6, 10 **2.** 7, 9, 7 **3.** 9, 3, 9
4. 8, 8, 9 **5.** 128, 96, 60, 84, 0
6. 48, 93, 88, 90, 65

Page 38
1. 68¢ **2.** 93¢ **3.** 44¢
4. 117¢ or $1.17

Page 39
1. $2.55 **2.** $16.06 **3.** $4.01
4. $2.84

Page 40
1. $4.85 **2.** $10.90 **3.** $62.10
4. $31.80 **5.** $19.85

Page 41
1. $1,672.19; $1,026.75; $356.77
2. $981.60; $180.00; $176.85
3. $9,166.69; $1,970.70; $9,633.24
4. $14,323.20; $73.85; $11,123.00
5. $3,007.45; $14,011.10; $242.44

Page 42 and Page 43
Least amount:
1 $5.00, 1 $1.00, 1 quarter, 1 dime,
1 nickel, 9 pennies, $6.49 total
Greatest amount:
3 $5.00, 3 $1.00, 5 quarters, 1 dime,
1 nickel, 1 penny, $19.41 total

Page 44
1. 17.22+5.00=22.22 Gina had $22.22.
2. 18.77-14.50=4.27 Matt would have $4.27 left.
3. 3.50+4.00+10.00=17.50 Jon got $17.50.
4. 87.00-53.00=34.00 Len needs $34.00 more.
5. 20.00+12.00=32.00 Dan has $32.00.
6. 18.00-6.00=12.00 Emma needs $12.00 more.

Page 45
1. $\frac{2}{4}$, $\frac{6}{8}$, $\frac{3}{9}$ **2.** $\frac{9}{15}$, $\frac{9}{18}$, $\frac{3}{24}$
3. $\frac{16}{36}$, $\frac{25}{40}$, $\frac{21}{49}$ **4.** $\frac{36}{45}$, $\frac{15}{21}$, $\frac{63}{72}$

Page 46
1. $\frac{3}{5}$, $\frac{5}{7}$ **2.** $\frac{11}{12}$, $\frac{7}{9}$ **3.** $\frac{19}{20}$, $\frac{13}{16}$
4. $\frac{2}{9}$, $\frac{8}{20}$ **5.** $\frac{4}{12}$, $\frac{7}{32}$ **6.** $\frac{10}{24}$, $\frac{2}{14}$

Page 47
1. 8,500; 6,712; 9,809; 9,080
2. 6,308; 13,046; 8,180; 11,055
3. 8,066; 11,195; 10,191; 9,809
4. 11,906; 7,600; 7,424; 11,039
5. 5,008; 10,087; 6,041; 11,817

Page 48
1. 4,406; 1,296; 2,067; 2,947
2. 4,728; 6,035; 3,760; 5,965
3. 3,559; 5,032; 4,802; 2,058
4. 19,909; 19,063; 21,879; 54,077
5. 40,696; 35,086; 10,274; 45,663

Page 49
1a. 2,479+3,210=5,689
5,689 people went to the concert.
1b. 3,210-2,479=731
731 more people attended on Saturday
night than Friday night.
2a. 1,324+1,129=2,453
2,453 graduated from the two high schools.
2b. 1,324-1,129=195
195 more students graduated from East High.
3a. 8,721-7,820=901
901 more people live in Littletown.
3b. 8,721+7,820=16,541
16,541 people live in the two towns.

Page 50
1. 6 **2.** 2, 3
3. 2, 4 **4.** 4, 2

Answer Pages

Page 51
1. $1\frac{1}{10}$ .1   **2.** $5\frac{5}{10}$ .5
3. $4\frac{4}{10}$ .4   **4.** $3\frac{3}{10}$ .3
5. $8\frac{8}{10}$ .8   **6.** $9\frac{9}{10}$ .9

Page 52
1. 48 squares should be shaded.
2. 73 squares should be shaded.
3. 31 squares should be shaded.
4. 17 squares should be shaded.
5. 69 squares should be shaded.
6. 24 squares should be shaded.

Page 53
1. 52, 62, 94,162, 146
2. 51, 69, 273, 216, 252
3. 216, 288, 380, 168, 228
4. 240, 165, 450, 360, 430
5. 96, 582, 246, 492, 462
6. 108, 138, 156, 325, 390

Page 54
1. 119, 133, 161, 322, 259
2. 504, 168, 736, 664, 376
3. 756, 243, 810, 513, 675
4. 720, 970, 360, 440, 850
5. 413, 608, 594, 590, 584

Page 55
1. 29x3=87   87 cookies
2. 12x7=84   84 inches
3. 17x6=102   102 miles
4. 48x7=336   336 pages
5. 50x5=250   250 trading cards
6. 73x4=292   292 stamps

Page 56
1. 30, 12, 40   **2.** 28, 40, 18
3. 36, 30, 36   **4.** 60, 60, 100
5. 40, 54, 0   **6.** 54, 0, 56

Page 57
1. 441, 195, 345, 576, 469
2. 385, 639, 420, 600, 304
3. 574, 510, 267, 747, 440
4. 630, 828, 768, 570, 396
5. 496, 553, 602, 470, 312

Page 58
1. 315, 273, 234   **2.** 212, 81, 152
3. 104, 162, 495   **4.** 84, 456, 276
5. 85, 174, 332   **6.** 60, 135, 140
7. 120, 54, 280

Page 59
Answers for totals will vary.
1. 10   **2.** 2   **3.** 2   **4.** 10
5. 2   **6.** 2   **7.** 2   **8.** 2

Page 60
1. 50, 60, 70; tens, 1
2. 600, 700, 800; hundreds, 1
3. 20, 25, 30; ones, 5
4. 85, 95, 105; tens, 1
5. 400, 300, 200; hundreds, 1
6. 6, 5, 4; ones, 1

Page 61
1. The mouse. It has the shortest bar on the graph.
2. The elephant. It has the longest bar on the graph.
3. The elephant. Its bar on the graph is a little longer than the human's bar.
4. mouse and elephant: about 75 years
lion and mouse: about 26 years
human and chinchilla: about 60 years

Answer Pages

Page 62
She should step on boards that are multiples of 4. For example, 4, 8, 12, 16, etc.

4, 8, 12, 16, 20, 24, 28, 32, 36, 40, 44, 48, 52, 56, 60, 64, 68, 72, 76, 80, 84, 88, 92, 96, 100, 104, 108, 112, 116, 120, 124, 128, 132, 136, 140, 144

Page 63
2	4	6	8	10
12	14	16	18	20
22	24	26	28	30
32	34	36	38	40
42	44	46	48	50

1	3	5	7	9
11	13	15	17	19
21	23	25	27	29
31	33	35	37	39
41	43	45	47	49

Answers will vary.

Page 64
148, 184, 418, 481
814, 841
148, 184
184, 418, 484
481, 814

573, 537, 735, 753
357, 375, 537, 573
735, 753
357, 375, 537
573, 735

Page 65
1. water spider, praying mantis, ladybug
2. 50
3. 300
4. praying mantis
5. 1,100

Page 66
crab, lobster, jellyfish, sea bass, shark, sponge, whale, octopus

octopus
Answers will vary.

Page 67
Matt has to travel 20 feet at 5 feet per second, or 20 ÷ 5 = 4 seconds to the finish line. Denise must travel 60 feet at 10 feet per second or 60 ÷ 10 = 6 seconds to the finish line. Matt wins the race.

Page 68
Lori is ten years old.
Allie is five years old.
If, in 5 years time Allie will be as old as Lori is now, and Lori is twice as old as Allie's age, you only need to multiply 5x2 or add 5+5 to find Lori's age. Then subtract 10-5 for Allie's age.

Page 69
The sum of the numbers above the line is 39.
The sum of the numbers below the line is 39.

Page 70 and Page 71
Across:

	1. 2,535	**2.** 550,450
3. 5,350	**4.** 76,472	**5.** 19,290
6. 2,400	**7.** 27,305	**8.** 37,496
Down:	**9.** 38,225	**10.** 1,146
11. 35,225	**12.** 72,400	**13.** 55,330
14. 4,220	**15.** 41,270	**16.** 72,090

Page 72
1. $\frac{2}{8}$ or $\frac{1}{4}$ 2. $\frac{4}{6}$ or $\frac{2}{3}$ 3. $\frac{2}{4}$ or $\frac{1}{2}$

4. $\frac{4}{12}$ or $\frac{1}{3}$ 5. $\frac{4}{8}$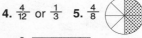

6. $\frac{8}{12}$

Page 73
Six of each coin.

Page 74
Grayson predicts number seven.